LANDMARK TOP TENS

The World's Most Amazing
Palaces

Ann Weil

Chicago, Illinois

www.heinemannraintree.com
Visit our website to find out
more information about
Heinemann-Raintree books.

To order:

☎ Phone 888-454-2279

🖥 Visit www.heinemannraintree.com
to browse our catalog and order online.

© 2012 Raintree
an imprint of Capstone Global Library, LLC
Chicago, Illinois

Customer Service: 888-454-2279
Visit our website at www.heinemannraintree.com

Edited by Megan Cotugno and Vaarunika Dharmapala
Designed by Victoria Allen
Picture research by Hannah Taylor and Ruth Blair
Illustrated by HL Studios and Oxford Designers
 and Illustrators
Original illustrations © Capstone Global Library Ltd (2011)
Production by Camilla Crask
Originated by Capstone Global Library Ltd
Printed in China by CTPS

15 14 13 12 11
10 9 8 7 6 5 4 3 2

Library of Congress Cataloging-in-Publication Data
Weil, Ann.
 The world's most amazing palaces / Ann Weil.—1st ed.
  p. cm.—(Landmark top tens)
 Includes bibliographical references and index.
 ISBN 978-1-4109-4237-1 (hc)—ISBN 978-1-4109-4248-7
(pbk.) 1. Palaces—Juvenile literature. I. Title.
 NA7710.W45 2011
 728.8'2—dc22   2010038397

Acknowledgments
The author and publishers are grateful to the following for
permission to reproduce copyright material: Alamy Images
p. 21 (© Images & Stories); Corbis pp. 17 (Michel Setboun), 19
(Craig Lovell), 23 (Gianni Dagli Orti), 27 (epa/Guo Xin); Getty
Images pp. 13 (AFP PHOTO/ROSLAN RAHMAN), 22 (De
Agostini Picture Library), 24 (AFP PHOTO/INTERPRESS/
ALEXANDER DROZDOV); istockphoto p. 20 (© Lebazele);
Photolibrary pp. 5 (Sabine Lubenow), 6 (View Stock), 11
(Britain on View/Pawel Libera), 14 (Age footstock), 16 (Brian
Lawrence), 18 (TAO Images); Rex Features p. 12 (Tim Rooke);
Shutterstock pp. 4 (© S.Borisov), 7 (© Hung Chung Chih), 8
(© Fillip Fuxa), 9 (© Jose Ignacio Soto), 10 (© Jozef Sedmak),
15 (© jbor), 26 (© Attila JÁNDI).

Cover photograph of Potala Palace in Tibet reproduced with
permission of Shutterstock (© enote).

We would like to thank Daniel Block for his invaluable help in
the preparation of this book.

Every effort has been made to contact copyright holders of
material reproduced in this book. Any omissions will be
rectified in subsequent printings if notice is given to the
publisher.

Contents

Some words are printed in bold, **like this**. You can find out what they mean in the glossary.

Palaces

A palace is a mansion built for a king, queen, or prince. As long as there has been royalty, there have been palaces. Palaces were more than large, splendid homes for a royal family. Kings or queens worked from their palace as well. Seated on an imposing throne, they might listen to advisers, sort out disputes, and hear news of their kingdom. Palaces were homes for nonroyals, too. Cooks, servants, and ladies-in-waiting all worked in palaces.

The Alhambra Palace in Spain includes part of an old fortress.

The building of the Doge's Palace in Venice, Italy, was started in 1340, but it has had many later additions.

Palaces today

Even now, palaces are among the grandest buildings in a country. A few, such as Buckingham Palace in London, England, remain royal **residences**. Some are used as government offices. Others, such as the Louvre in Paris, were turned into museums. Whatever their uses, palaces are still some of the most amazing buildings in the world.

The Forbidden City

The Forbidden City in China is the largest palace **complex** in the world! There are 800 different buildings separated by vast open courtyards. It was the home of Chinese emperors from the 1400s. The emperors lived a sheltered life inside the **Imperial** Palace, which was surrounded by the old walled capital city, now known as Beijing.

Visitors passed through a series of gates before reaching the formal entrance to the Forbidden City.

Permission Granted!

This amazing palace complex is no longer "forbidden." It is now a museum and open to the public.

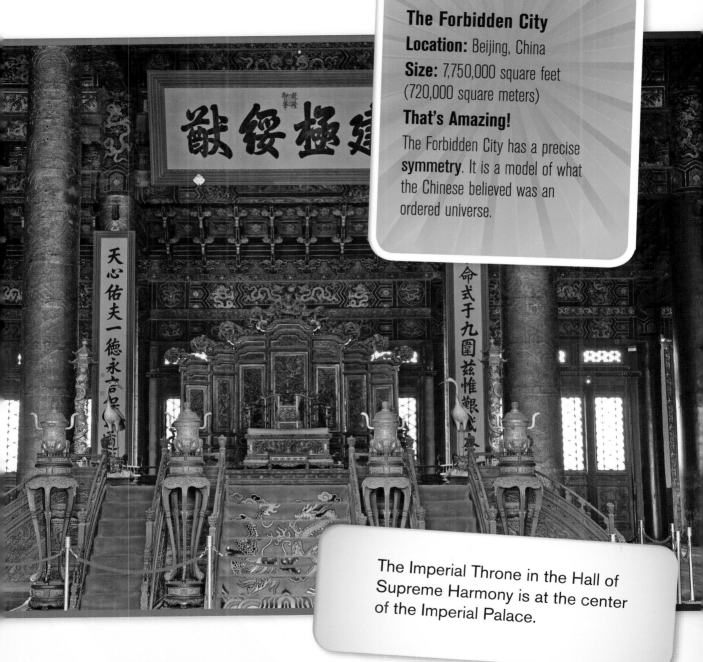

The Forbidden City

Location: Beijing, China

Size: 7,750,000 square feet (720,000 square meters)

That's Amazing!
The Forbidden City has a precise **symmetry**. It is a model of what the Chinese believed was an ordered universe.

The Imperial Throne in the Hall of Supreme Harmony is at the center of the Imperial Palace.

End of the emperors

In 1911 there was a **revolution** in China. From that time on, emperors no longer ruled China. The last of the emperors was a young child at that time. The new Chinese government let him live in the Forbidden City until 1924.

7

Versailles

This amazing palace **complex** in France began as a royal hunting lodge in the country village of Versailles. Then King Louis XIV of France made it into one of the largest and most spectacular palaces in history. The transformation began in 1661. The king wanted grand apartments for himself and the queen. He also wanted homes at Versailles for various members of the French government. The project almost **bankrupted** the **state**!

The incredible gardens at Versailles are almost the same as they were in the time of Louis XIV.

Royal court

The royal **court** was officially established at Versailles in 1682. Louis continued to add on to Versailles during his lifetime. Following the French **Revolution** in the late 1700s, Versailles was no longer the center of government, but it remains the most **opulent**, luxurious palace in history.

The Hall of Mirrors is the most dazzling room at Versailles. It was designed to impress visitors to the palace.

Versailles
Location: Versailles, France
Size: 721,206 square feet (67,002 square meters)
That's Amazing!
This palace is a symbol of "absolute monarchy," when the ruler had total political power.

Buckingham Palace

In the early 1700s the Duke of Buckingham built Buckingham House as a grand London home. In 1761 King George III bought Buckingham House for his wife, Queen Charlotte, to use as a family home. Buckingham House became Buckingham Palace in the 1820s during the reign of George IV. Queen Victoria moved there in 1837 and made it her official **residence**.

Buckingham Palace
Location: London, United Kingdom
Size: 828,818 square feet (77,000 square meters)

That's Amazing!
Buckingham Palace is the world's largest "working" royal palace.

On special occasions, the royal family appears on the balcony beneath the central pillars of Buckingham Palace.

The world's largest workplace?

Like many European palaces, most of Buckingham Palace is used for administrative and **state** purposes. Today more than 800 members of staff are based in Buckingham Palace, including housekeepers, gardeners, cooks, and even a clockmaker!

Inside The Palace

There are 1,514 doors and 760 windows in Buckingham Palace. It also has 775 rooms, 19 state rooms, 52 royal and guest bedrooms, 188 staff bedrooms, 92 offices, and 78 bathrooms!

The Changing of the Guard is a well-known ceremony at Buckingham Palace.

Istana Nurul Iman

Istana Nurul Iman is the official **residence** of the **Sultan** of Brunei. Its name is Arabic for "palace of the light of faith" or "palace of the faith light." It was built in 1984 and cost more than $350 million!

Istana Nurul Iman

Location: Brunei (on the island of Borneo in Southeast Asia)

Size: 2,152,782 square feet (200,000 square meters)

That's Amazing!
It is the world's largest residential palace in use today.

Islam

The population of Brunei is about two-thirds **Muslim**. Muslim people follow the religion of Islam. Islam is the second largest world religion after **Christianity**.

The Sultan's palace has 1,788 rooms, 257 bathrooms, five swimming pools, and a **mosque** that can hold as many as 1,500 people. It even has air-conditioned stables for 200 ponies.

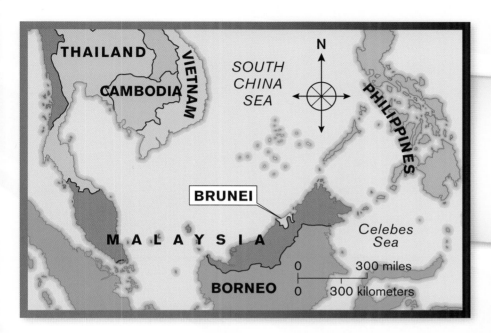

Brunei is a small country, but the Sultan's palace is the largest home in the world!

The throne hall of the palace was the setting for Sultan Hassanal Bolkiah's 60th birthday celebration in 2006.

Royal Palace of Madrid

King Juan Carlos and the royal family of Spain do not live in the Royal Palace of Madrid. Instead, it is used for **state** functions and ceremonies. The palace is on the same site as Alcazar, a medieval fortress that burned down on Christmas Day in 1734.

Royal Palace of Madrid
Location: Madrid, Spain
Size: 1,453,122 square feet (135,000 square meters)
That's Amazing!
It is the largest royal palace in western Europe.

The design for this massive rectangular building was based on the palace of Versailles.

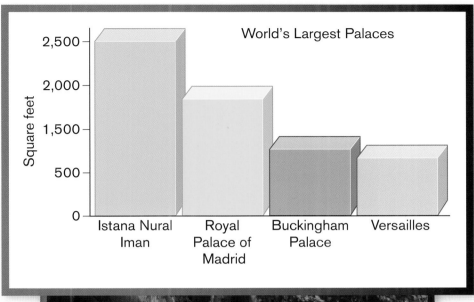

World's Largest Palaces

White marble statues of former kings and queens of Spain line the Plaza de Oriente of the palace.

The new palace

Construction of the new palace began a year after the fire. It took 26 years to build. This time builders used local limestone and granite to avoid the same fate for this royal palace. Visitors can tour 50 of the 2,800 rooms. The palace includes more than 40 balconies, parade grounds, and a large park.

Prince's Palace of Monaco

The Prince's Palace of Monaco started out as a fortress. It was built in 1191 by the **Republic** of Genoa. The powerful Grimaldi family captured the fortress in 1297. They ruled the area first as **feudal lords**, then as **sovereign** princes. The Grimaldi are still the royal family of Monaco today.

Prince's Palace of Monaco
Location: Principality of Monaco
That's Amazing!
The same family has ruled Monaco from this palace for more than 700 years!

Monaco
Unlike other European royals, the Grimaldi family ruled only a small area of land. Monaco is the second smallest country in the world (after the Vatican City).

Turbulent times

From 1005 to1797 Genoa was an independent **state** in what is now Italy. These were not all peaceful years. This is one of the few palaces in Europe to be **fortified** in order to protect the royal family from attack. In the 18th century the French seized the palace, forcing the Grimaldi family into **exile** for 20 years.

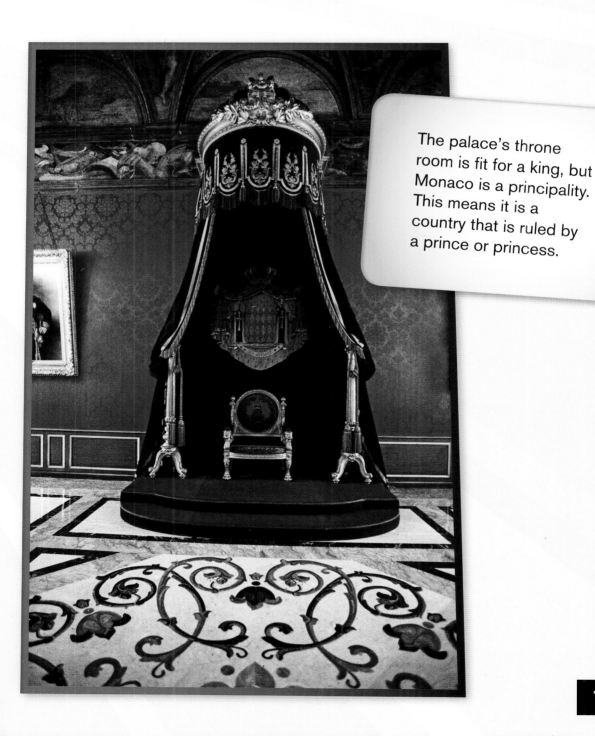

The palace's throne room is fit for a king, but Monaco is a principality. This means it is a country that is ruled by a prince or princess.

Potala Palace

In 637 CE the first emperor of Tibet built the Potala Palace on top of Red Mountain. He was to be married, and he needed a new home fit for his Chinese princess bride. His amazing palace had 1,000 rooms!

The Potala Palace has two parts. The Red Palace is at the center, with the White Palace as its wings.

Potala Palace
Location: Lhasa, Tibet (China)
Size: 1,399,308 square feet (130,000 square meters)
That's Amazing!
It is the highest palace in the world.

Dalai Lama

The fifth Dalai Lama built the modern palace in 1645. The Dalai Lama is a spiritual leader for the people of Tibet, who are **Buddhist**. He is also the head of their government. The palace was a home for the Dalai Lama and his large staff. It was also a religious school.

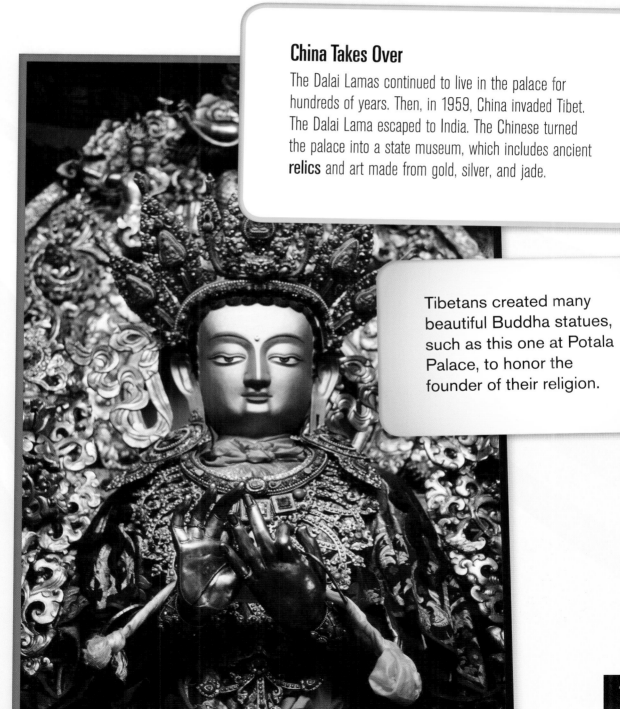

China Takes Over

The Dalai Lamas continued to live in the palace for hundreds of years. Then, in 1959, China invaded Tibet. The Dalai Lama escaped to India. The Chinese turned the palace into a state museum, which includes ancient **relics** and art made from gold, silver, and jade.

Tibetans created many beautiful Buddha statues, such as this one at Potala Palace, to honor the founder of their religion.

19

Topkapi Palace

In 1453 a 23-year-old **sultan** conquered the Roman city of Constantinople. He changed the name of the city to Istanbul and made it the capital of his mighty Ottoman Empire. Then he ordered a new palace to be built where the ancient Greeks (who controlled the city before the Romans) had built their **acropolis**. For nearly four centuries (1465–1853) Topkapi Palace was the main government center for the entire Ottoman Empire.

Topkapi Palace was the home of the sultans of the Ottoman Empire. In 1924 it was turned into a religious museum.

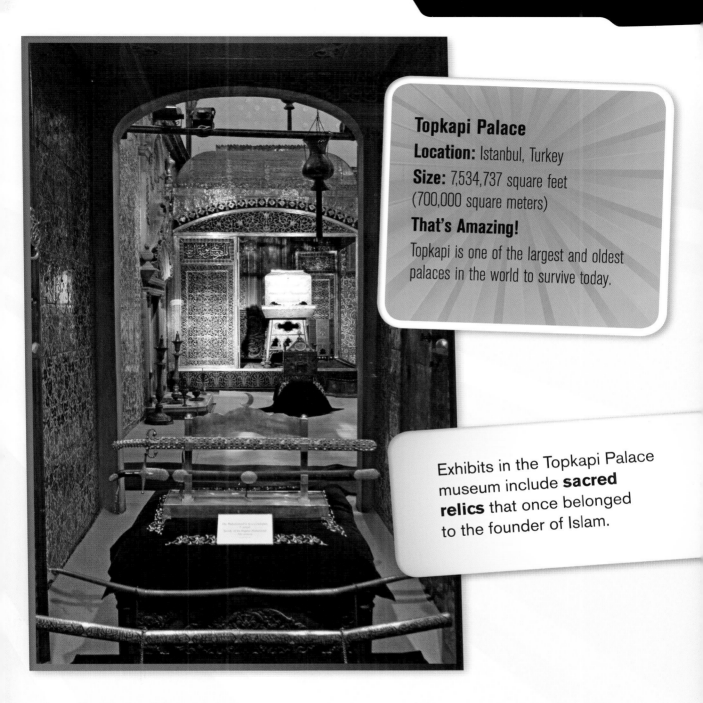

Topkapi Palace
Location: Istanbul, Turkey
Size: 7,534,737 square feet
(700,000 square meters)
That's Amazing!
Topkapi is one of the largest and oldest palaces in the world to survive today.

Exhibits in the Topkapi Palace museum include **sacred relics** that once belonged to the founder of Islam.

A fortress palace

Protective walls surrounded the palace, which had four main courtyards. Offices were in the outer court of this fortress palace. The inner court included space for royal **pavilions**, the palace school, and the **harem**. The palace **complex** eventually included **mosques**, a hospital, bakeries, and a **mint**.

Knossos

There were many palaces in ancient Greece, but Knossos on the island of Crete was the most amazing. King Minos ruled a large kingdom from this huge palace. There were hundreds of decorated rooms and grand staircases. Vast storerooms were filled with olive oil, grain, and wine that people sent as payment for their taxes.

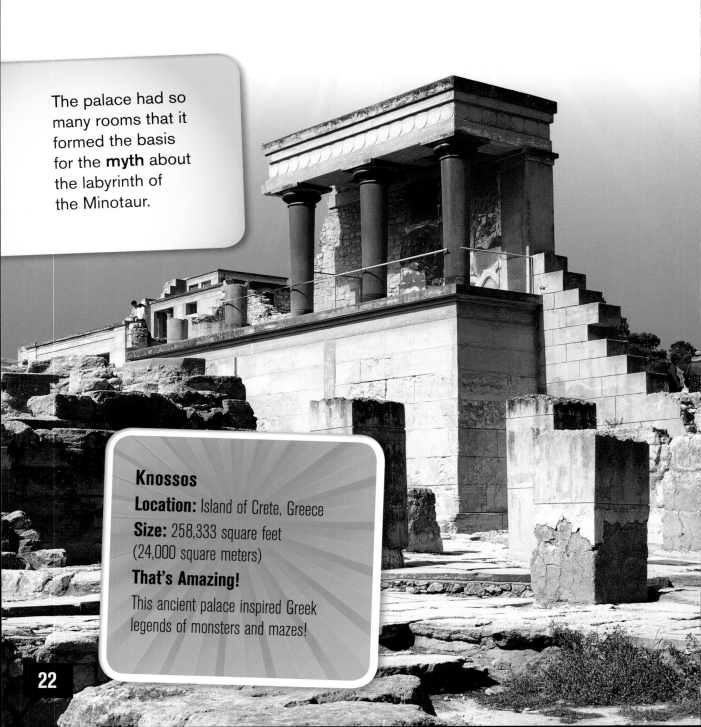

The palace had so many rooms that it formed the basis for the **myth** about the labyrinth of the Minotaur.

Knossos

Location: Island of Crete, Greece

Size: 258,333 square feet (24,000 square meters)

That's Amazing!

This ancient palace inspired Greek legends of monsters and mazes!

Myth of the Minotaur

An ancient Greek myth tells how every year 14 teenagers were **sacrificed** to a monster called the Minotaur. They entered a giant underground maze, called the labyrinth. The victims became lost in the maze, and the Minotaur ate them. A prince decided he would kill the Minotaur. He unrolled string as he made his way into the labyrinth. After he found and killed the Minotaur, he followed the string out of the maze.

The Minotaur was a mythical monster, a gruesome half-man, half-bull that lived in the labyrinth.

Ice Palace

The first Ice Palace was built in Russia in 1740. An empress named Anna played a cruel joke on a nobleman she did not like. First she forced him to marry against his will. Then he and his bride had to spend the night in a "honeymoon suite" inside the ice palace. The unhappy couple might have frozen to death if the bride had not traded her pearl necklace for the guard's sheepskin coat!

Ice Palace
Location: St. Petersburg, Russia
Size: 980 square feet
(91 square meters)
That's Amazing!
The Ice Palace had ice furniture, including an ice bed with an ice mattress and pillows.

Incredible ice

In 2006 a Russian art center built a copy of the ice palace. The design was based on descriptions of the original ice palace in historical documents. Huge ice blocks were "glued" together with water. When it was finished it looked as if it were cut from a single block of ice. Frozen sculptures in the shapes of trees, animals, and birds surrounded this amazing palace. Actors in historical costumes re-created the "amusing wedding" that took place 266 years before.

More than three tons of ice was taken from nearby lakes to make this 20-foot high copy of the ice palace.

Palaces in Danger

Over time, earthquakes and other natural disasters have demolished ancient palaces. The palace at Knossos in Crete was destroyed by an earthquake, rebuilt, and then destroyed again by fire. Natural disasters are still a threat to palaces. Throughout history, palaces have also been destroyed during wars. Some of the largest palaces of the Islamic world are in the wartorn country of Iraq. These palaces are in great danger until peace comes to this region.

The beautiful Azem Palace in Damascus, Syria, is now a museum and a **World Heritage Site**. This protects it from falling into ruin.

The Chinese government completed an underpass beneath Potala Palace in 2010 at a cost of $5.5 million.

The threat to Potala Palace

Recently Potala Palace in Tibet has been in danger because of **renovations** being carried out by the Chinese government. The first stages of these renovations seriously damaged traditional artworks. Now the Chinese government has built a new underpass in the front courtyard of Potala Palace. Work on this began in 2009. It triggered a flood that created cracks, which put the entire palace in danger.

Palaces Facts and Figures

Throughout history kings and queens have built amazing homes for themselves and their royal families. Some palaces were also the center of a country's government. Which palace do you think is the most amazing?

The Forbidden City

Location: Beijing, China

Size: 7,750,000 square feet (720,000 square meters)

That's Amazing!

The Forbidden City has a precise symmetry. It is a model of what the Chinese believed was an ordered universe.

Versailles

Location: Versailles, France

Size: 721,206 square feet (67,002 square meters)

That's Amazing!

This palace is a symbol of "absolute monarchy," when the ruler had total political power.

Buckingham Palace

Location: London, United Kingdom

Size: 828,818 square feet (77,000 square meters)

That's Amazing!

Buckingham Palace is the world's largest "working" royal palace.

Istana Nurul Iman

Location: Brunei (on the island of Borneo in Southeast Asia)

Size: 2,152,782 square feet (200,000 square meters)

That's Amazing!

It is the world's largest residential palace in use today.

Royal Palace of Madrid

Location: Madrid, Spain

Size: 1,453,122 square feet (135,000 square meters)

That's Amazing!

It is the largest royal palace in western Europe.

Prince's Palace of Monaco

Location: Principality of Monaco

That's Amazing!

The same family has ruled Monaco from this palace for more than 700 years!

Potala Palace

Location: Lhasa, Tibet (China)

Size: 1,399,308 square feet (130,000 square meters)

That's Amazing!

It is the highest palace in the world.

Topkapi Palace

Location: Istanbul, Turkey

Size: 7,534,737 square feet (700,000 square meters)

That's Amazing!

Topkapi is one of the largest and oldest palaces in the world to survive today.

Knossos

Location: Island of Crete, Greece

Size: 258,333 square feet (24,000 square meters)

That's Amazing!

This ancient palace inspired Greek legends of monsters and mazes!

Ice Palace

Location: St. Petersburg, Russia

Size: 980 square feet (91 square meters)

That's Amazing!

The Ice Palace had ice furniture, including an ice bed with an ice mattress and pillows.

Glossary

acropolis ancient Greek fortress that also served as the religious center of the city

bankrupt run out of money

Buddhist someone who follows Buddhism, a world religion that originated in India around 500 BCE

Christian someone who follows the religion based on the teachings of Jesus Christ

court group of people who attend to a king or queen

complex a set of buildings with a common use or purpose

exile forbidden to live in your home country

feudal lords noble landowners in medieval Europe

fortified made stronger to withstand an enemy attack

harem separate living space for a sultan's wives

imperial to do with an emperor or empire

Islamic to do with the Muslim religion that was founded by the prophet Muhammad

mint place where coins for money are made

mosque building where Muslim people worship

Muslim someone who follows the religion of Islam

myth story about ancient gods, heroes, or monsters

opulent expensive and showy or flashy

pavilion small, open building, often used for entertaining, with a roof for shelter but no walls

relic something from the past that survived when the rest is gone

renovations changes and additions to a place to make it bigger, better, or more modern

residence place where a family lives, such as a home or apartment

republic country that is ruled by a government rather than a king or queen

revolution battle to overthrow a ruler or government

sacred connected with religion

sacrifice to give up something valuable, such as one's own life

sovereign another word for ruler, such as a king or queen

state area with its own government that controls most of its own dealings

sultan king of a Muslim country

symmetry looks the same on both sides of an imaginary central line through the object, like the wings of a butterfly

World Heritage Site place with outstanding historical value

Books

Gallagher, Debbie. *Palaces, Mansions, and Castles*. North Mankato, Minn.: Smart Apple Media, 2008.

Knox, Barbara. *Forbidden City: China's Imperial Palace*. New York, NY: Bearport, 2006.

Mason, Anthony. *Versailles*. Milwaukee, Wis.: World Almanac Library, 2005.

Scarre, Christopher and Rebecca Stefoff. *The Palace of Minos at Knossos*. New York, NY: Oxford University Press, 2003.

Websites

http://www.royal.gov.uk/virtualtours/Flash%20Panoramas/flash_003.html
Take a virtual tour of Buckingham Palace!

http://en.chateauversailles.fr/homepage
Visit this website for more photos and information about the spectacular palace in Versailles, France.

Index